Dragons Breath & The Magic of Tapping

By

Linda Graham

and

Penny Rush

Artwork by Linda Graham

Dragons Breath & The Magic of Tapping

ISBN 978-0-9926630-1-8

First Edition

Winterbone Publishing

Bury St Edmunds, Suffolk UK
www.winterbone.co.uk

Printed in the UK for Winterbone Publishing by
Indigo Ross Design & Print Ltd, Sudbury Suffolk

Dragons Breath & The Magic of Tapping

By

Linda Graham

and

Penny Rush

Dedicated to

Eligh, Rhys, Alisha,

Sam, Kigh, Joe,

Ella, Roxy, Zach,

Bella, Jack, Stan,

Daisy, Illia

Amy, Livvy & Lawrence

And to all the children of our world

Acknowledgements

We would like to give our thanks to our families and friends for their support and encouragement during the process of breathing and tapping this book into life. Many thanks go to Marie and Kevin Winterbone for their patience and help with editing our book.

Contents

"If you want your children to be intelligent,

read them fairy tales.

If you want them to be more intelligent,

read them more fairy tales."

Albert Einstein

Dragons Breath

The High Priestess' story about Dragons Breath
by

Linda Graham

Dragons Breath

A very long time ago, nestled in a valley between two steep hills, there was a village called Peace Valley. The people of the village all helped each other.

In Potters Lane, a boy called Harry lived with his parents. He had many friends in Peace Valley, although his best friend was Lily, who lived with her parents in Swan Cottage, in the High Street.

Now Peace Valley was quite unusual because it had two very interesting people living there.

On top of one hill, lived a very wise High Priestess, with Breeze her friendly dragon. She was always doing something mystical and often would be deep in thought, talking to herself.

On the top of the other hill, lived the very magical Fairy Godmother with her clever dog Molly. She was always doing something with her magic and giggled happily.

Now, these two ladies were great friends, and often met for tea and cake. They were both always on hand to help anyone in the village, if needed.   Everyone in Peace Valley knew they could just ask and help would be there.

The High Priestess helped to teach the people in the village how to be mindful, how to be calmer and many other things.

Most of the time all of the children in Peace Valley were happy and enjoyed playing together. Sometimes though, they would get cross about things and stamp their feet.

Sometimes some of the children got worried about things. Sometimes they felt sad. Sometimes they argued with each other. Of course, this does happen to everyone from time to time.

One day the High Priestess was sitting in her garden, when she heard some of the village children arguing again. Then she heard some of the children shouting at each other and others joining in.

"Hmmm, interesting," said the High Priestess to Breeze, "they don't sound very happy, do they?" Breeze looked up and could see the High Priestess was thinking about how she could help the children. "I know," she said suddenly, "We will invite all the children to come here and learn about Dragons Breath."

The High Priestess wrote out her notice and then
she rode down to the village on the back of Breeze.

Invitation
Saturday 7th at 10.30am
Children of Peace Valley you
are all invited to my home to
learn all about
DRAGONS BREATH
It is very good for making you
feel happy inside.
Afterwards there will be cakes
and fruit juice.
Love High Priestess

She put the invitation on the notice board, in the
middle of the village for everyone to see. Very
soon, everyone in Peace Valley knew about the
invitation and all the parents said that the children
could go.

It was a sunny day that Saturday morning when all the parents took the children up the hill to the High Priestess.

After all of the children had stroked Breeze's head, they sat in a circle around him in the lovely garden. Breeze went fast asleep, curled up next to the High Priestess.

The High Priestess asked, "Are you ready to learn about Dragons Breath?"

All of the children shouted out, "Yes we are ready!" and they really were. Everyone was curious, wondering what Dragons Breath was all about.

The High Priestess explained, "To be your best self, you can use Dragons Breath to help you, especially when you feel cross or angry." She looked down at her sleeping dragon and gently stroked his head.

"One day," she said, "I noticed Breeze taking a great big breath in and after he breathed it all out, he had such a huge smile. Hmmm... I said to myself, I'm going to try that. So I did. Just like this..." and the High Priestess breathed in a very, very long way and then she breathed out. Her smile was huge! "Ooh I feel lovely inside," she said.

The High Priestess told the children that she talked with Breeze for a very long time. He explained all there was to know about Dragons Breath and she practised with Breeze every day. She found out that even if she felt a bit sad, when she did the Dragons Breath, she felt much better. After three Dragons Breaths she soon found her smile again.

The High Priestess instructed the children, "Take in a really deep breath and now breathe it all the way out." After they had done this, everyone was smiling and two of the children, Harry and Lily, were giggling together.

The High Priestess smiled at Harry and Lily and said, "When we breathe more deeply we find our smiles. Then everyone around us feels good as well." Everyone was smiling and feeling relaxed. They liked the High Priestess and they loved Breeze, who was still asleep by her side.

The High Priestess said, "There is much more to learn about Dragons Breath." Then she looked at the circle of children and said, "Put your hands up, if you had lots of smiles this week." She looked around the group and was dismayed that only three children had put their hands up.

"Now put your hand up if you have felt sad or cross or angry." All the children put their hands up.

"Oh my goodness, I was right, you all need the Dragons Breath. Would you like to tell me what has made you sad, cross and angry?"

As the children knew that she was very kind, they all began to tell the High Priestess about their arguments, being sad, being cross and even stamping their feet.

She listened very carefully and then said, "Oh bless you all."

The High Priestess said, "Come on let's do a great exercise. Close your eyes and take a really deep breath in, and then breathe out."

"Now we are going to do that again. Close your eyes children. I want you to think about all those things that made you sad or cross. Are you thinking of them?" she asked as she looked at the children's faces. They all nodded.

"Keep on thinking about those things and take a really deep breath all the way in."

The High Priestess breathed in deeply with them and said, "And breathe out. Breathe in deeply one more time, keep thinking about all those things that made you sad or cross. Breathe all the way in and out. Now open your eyes."

Harry and Lily started giggling and some of the other children joined in until everyone was laughing.

"How do you feel about all those things that made you sad or cross?" the High Priestess asked. "Put your hand up if you forgot about them." Quite a few of them put their hands up, including Harry and Lily who were still giggling. "Put your hand up if those things don't seem so bad now." All the children put their hands up and were smiling and nodding to each other.

The High Priestess asked, "Shall we do another great exercise?"

"Oh Yes!" the children said excitedly.

"This is called Grounding," she explained, "Would you all stand up for me please?" and everyone stood up. The dragon lifted his sleepy head, yawned and closed his eyes going back to sleep again.

"Now I want you all to pretend you are a tree. Stretch your arms up into the air like branches and imagine you are growing tree roots into the ground." The children stretched their arms and imagined roots growing into the hill.

"That's wonderful, well done everyone," said the High Priestess. "Now let's sit down again. Do you feel like you are all growing out of the hill now?" asked the High Priestess.

"Yes!" the children shouted joyfully.

The dragon snored a little in his sleep and the children giggled.

The High Priestess stroked his head.

"Now we are getting very close to understanding the Dragons Breath. You all know that if you take in three very deep breaths everything seems better. This is how it all works. When we breathe in, we take in a life force that helps us to live. The more we breathe in the happier we are."

The High Priestess unrolled a big piece of paper and laid it down in the centre of the circle. On the paper was a drawing of five steps.

5 Dragons Breath

4

3

2

1

The High Priestess said, "We can take lots of different breaths. Each breath connects with a different step and has a different meaning." She pointed to the diagram at the first step and explained:

Step 1. Is where we take a tiny breath when we are worried or afraid

Step 2. Here our breath is a bit bigger and is when we think deeply about our feelings

Step 3. Now our breath is a bit bigger again and here we can be strong minded and determined

Step 4. Our deep breaths here are where we find all of our smiles

Step 5. This breath is very deep and is where we use Dragons Breath. We pull in a very deep breath and make a big noise as we breathe out

The children laughed and the High Priestess smiled. "Let's do the breathing steps up to Dragons Breath. It's a lot of fun. Now close your eyes. Are you ready?" asked the High Priestess and the children nodded to say yes.

"Let's do step one. I want you to imagine you are playing a game and you are hiding from your friend. He is looking for you and is really close to you. He's getting closer every moment, he's getting closer and now has nearly found you." The High Priestess paused and then asked, "Can you feel that your breath is very small?"

"Now open your eyes. This is the first step, where you have only a tiny breath or you are holding in your breath. You don't feel very calm, do you?"

"Now step two, close your eyes and imagine it is the night before your birthday and you are in bed, trying to get to sleep. You are so excited thinking about your birthday."

The High Priestess paused and then said, "Open your eyes. Did you feel that your breathing became very quick as you thought about your birthday? This is what happens to our breathing when we are excited."

"Now step three, close your eyes and imagine you are getting ready to race across the playground and you really, really want to win." The High Priestess paused and then said, "Open your eyes. Did you feel that your breathing became very strong in your tummy?"

"Step four, close your eyes and imagine that your favourite food is in front of you. Mmmm... it smells delicious."

The High Priestess paused and then said, "Open your eyes. Did you feel yourself taking in delicious breaths? This is because thinking about delicious food makes you smile. When you smile you automatically breathe to the fourth step."

"We are now at step five, where we find Dragons Breath," said the High Priestess. "If you are ever feeling really cross about something, you can do the Dragons Breath and you will feel so much better."

Just then Breeze woke up, raised his head and yawned. "Did someone call me?" he asked.

"Oh hello Breeze, would you like to demonstrate step five of the Dragons Breath?" asked the High Priestess.

The dragon stretched, yawned and said, "Oh yes I would. I love the Dragons Breath."

He stood up, swishing his tail. "Hello children. Let me tell you how to use my favourite part of Dragons Breath." Breeze shook himself awake.

"If you ever feel cross or sad or angry, all you need to
do, is take in the very deepest breath you can and
then push the air out with a great big noise, like this!"

The dragon took a very deep breath and roared out
his breath. "Aaaaaaaarrrrhhhh," and then he grinned.
All the children laughed and clapped their hands.
They loved Breeze and he loved the children as well.

Breeze laughed with the children. He asked, "Who wants to do the Dragons Breath?"

Harry and Lily jumped up and both said, "Me!" at the same time.

"Ok, excellent!" said the dragon. "Take a deep breath in and roar it out."

Harry and Lily took in a really deep breath and roared loudly, "Aaaaaaarrrrrhhhhh!" and then they laughed and laughed. All the children laughed as well.

"Come on children," said the High Priestess. "Up you jump and everyone do the Dragons Breath."

Breeze grinned at them all. "Now take a really deep breath in. Now roar it out, aaaaaaarrrrrhhhhh!" That is just what they did. And they all laughed and laughed.

"Who can answer this question children?" asked the High Priestess. "Whenever you feel cross, angry or sad w hat could you do to make yourself feel better?"

Harry shouted out "Do the Dragons Breath!" and with that he took a deep breath and roared "aaaaarrrrrhhhhh!"

The rest of the children joined in and faced each other roaring like dragons.

They all felt brilliant, smiley and very, very happy.

The High Priestess smiled and then asked, "If we are only taking a small breath and we are on step one, what does that mean?"

"We are frightened!" called out several children.

The High Priestess said, "If we are frightened and we breathe up to step four, what will happen?"

"We will find our smiles again," called out Harry.

"And we are not afraid anymore," added Lily.

"If we breathe a little more to the second step, we keep on thinking about our sad thoughts, so we keep on feeling sad," said the High Priestess. "What step do we need to breathe to find our smiles again?"

"Step four!" shouted all the children.

"Well done!" said the High Priestess. "Everyone breathe to the fourth step now," she encouraged. So all the children breathed to the fourth step and very quickly everyone found their smile there.

5 Dragons Breath

"Now children," said Breeze, "Whenever you feel cross, angry or sad what could you do to make yourself feel better?"

Harry shouted out, "Do the Dragons Breath," and with that he took a deep breath and roared "aaaaarrrrhhhhh!"

The rest of the children joined in and faced each other roaring like dragons. They all felt brilliant, smiley and very, very happy.

After some yummy cakes and fruit juice the parents came to take the children home. They waved goodbye to the High Priestess and Breeze.

The High Priestess listened as they roared their way back down into the village. For most of the time Peace Valley was very peaceful and settled. Dragons Breath was such a winner for a smiling heart and happy face.

And with good breathing skills they lived happily ever after.

The Magic of Tapping

The Fairy Godmother's story about Magical Tapping

by

Penny Rush

The Magic of Tapping

Once upon a time in a land far, far away there was a village called Peace Valley. The people of the village knew all their neighbours, they were very friendly and helped each other.

In Potters Lane, a boy called Harry lived with his parents. He had many friends in Peace Valley, although his best friend was Lily, who lived with her parents in Swan Cottage, in the High Street.

The people of the village knew all their neighbours, they were very friendly and helped each other.

Now Peace Valley was quite unusual, because it had two interesting people living there. On one hill a High Priestess lived there with her pet dragon, Breeze.

On the other hill across the valley lived a Fairy Godmother with her dog Molly. Now these two ladies were great friends, often meeting for tea and biscuits and were always on hand to help their fellow villagers if needed.

One day a big black cloud arrived over Peace Valley and it changed something about the people in the village. Some were feeling sad and fed up, others were worrying about things they didn't normally care about. Some people felt angry and wanted to argue with everyone and anything but couldn't understand why. Luckily for Peace Valley the wind came and blew the cloud away however the feelings of sadness, worry and anger remained.

Harry woke up one morning and was getting ready for school, his Mum was shouting at him for not being ready on time and this made him feel very angry, he felt like shouting back.

Harry stayed feeling angry until he got to school and still couldn't understand why he felt so cross inside.

Strangely when Lily woke up that morning she felt different too. She hadn't been able to sleep very well that night and she had these feelings inside that made her feel scared and worried and she couldn't understand why.

She told her Mum about how she was feeling. However her Mum was really busy getting all the packed lunches ready for the family and wasn't listening properly. So poor Lily set off for school still feeling the same.

When Harry and Lily were at school things just didn't get any better. So they talked to each other after school about what a rubbish day they had both had and couldn't understand why.

As they were walking back home Lily had a bright idea. She suddenly remembered the Fairy Godmother had always said to her, "If Mummy is too busy because she has so much to do, you can always come and see me!"

Harry and Lily said, "Let's go and see the Fairy Godmother, she'll know what to do to make us feel better," as Harry didn't want these angry feelings anymore and Lily definitely didn't like not being able to sleep because she felt sad and worried.

So off they went up the hill to see the Fairy Godmother and her little dog, Molly.

When they arrived the Fairy Godmother was so pleased to see them and so was Molly, her magical dog.

However, the Fairy Godmother could tell something wasn't quite right. She invited them in and asked them how she could help. So Lily and Harry sat down and told her about their feelings and how they didn't like them, and didn't know what to do about them. Well of course, the Fairy Godmother knew a thing or two about these feelings because she was such a wise woman.

She asked them to describe how these feelings first started, where they could feel them in their bodies and if these feelings had a colour. Harry thought this was all a bit silly and Lily wasn't sure that the Fairy Godmother really knew what she was talking about! However they knew she was very wise and kind so carried on listening.

Just then Molly went over to the children and put her paw on Lily's hand and gently patted it. The Fairy Godmother smiled to herself and said, "Yes Molly, you're quite right we need to do some tapping."

The Fairy Godmother then started tapping her wand on the side of her hand and asked the children to copy her using their first two fingers. First of all she talked to Harry, "Now Harry keep tapping your hand and tell me where you can feel all that anger in you." Harry replied, "It's in my tummy."

"Ok," said the Fairy Godmother, "And if it had a colour, what colour would it be?"

"Red," said Harry.

"Ok," said the Fairy Godmother, "Now Harry I want you to follow me as I tap on some points around my face. That's right, copy me and while we do that we're going to repeat these words." So whilst she tapped on the side of her hand she said, "Even though I have this anger inside me I'm really ok," she said this three times.

Harry followed although he thought she was really strange but he did like her so carried on. Then the Fairy Godmother started tapping some points on her face and said, "All this red anger in my tummy," and kept saying this while she tapped on points on the top of her head, near the inside of her eyebrow, the side of her eye, under her eye, under her nose, the middle of her chin and just below her collar bone and finally under her arm. And as she continued to tap all those points on her face, the Fairy Godmother also said, "I choose to let go of all this anger."

Well Harry thought this was really odd but whilst they were doing this he noticed that he wasn't feeling as angry. And after doing this a few times he noticed that the red feeling of anger in his tummy had completely gone! How magic was that!

Lily had watched this and could see how Harry's face had changed from a cross face to a happy one and she couldn't wait to try this herself.

So when the Fairy Godmother asked her. "Where do you feel the sadness and worry in you?"

She said, "It's around my heart."

"Has it got a colour?" the Fairy Godmother asked.

Lily said, "I'm not sure."

The Fairy Godmother said, "Just guess, it's fine to do that." Lily guessed it was a purple colour. Again the Fairy Godmother started tapping on the side of her hand and said, "Even though I have these sad feelings I'm ok."

She did this again three times. Then she started tapping around her face on all the same places as before and said, "These purple feelings of sadness in my heart," and she continued to tap all those points on her face and then said, "I choose to let go of all this sadness."

And just like Harry, Lily started to notice that she was feeling better and wasn't feeling so sad anymore – it was just like magic!

All those horrid feelings of being angry or sad had just disappeared!! The children were so amazed and asked the Fairy Godmother if she had used some magic. The Fairy Godmother replied, "Of course it wasn't my magic. You were tapping into your own magic and that's what sent those horrid feelings away."

The Fairy Godmother explained, "If you ever start to have those bad feelings, that make you feel angry or sad or frightened, you can use your magic by tapping just as I have shown you."

Harry and Lily were really excited. They couldn't wait to go and tell their Mummy and Daddy about this clever magic that we all have. Before they left the Fairy Godmother gave them a diagram of where to tap into their magic.

The next day Harry and Lily went into school and told their friends all about their new found magic. Some of the children didn't believe them, some did and some weren't sure. Harry and Lily smiled at each other, they knew how this had made them feel better. They had also noticed how everything seemed easier since tapping into their magic. The Fairy Godmother had told them, when they are feeling happy, good things stick to them like glue! And it was true!

They also found, that as they felt nice inside, it was impossible to be mean and nasty to anyone. Harry and Lily also began to understand that when someone else was being mean or spiteful it was because that person was feeling horrid inside. Those people really needed to find that special magic in themselves.

After a few weeks all the children in school started to notice that Harry and Lily were always much happier. They wanted to be happy as well so they asked them to teach them how to tap into their own magic. This made their school a great place to be, with everyone being kind to each other. They were having lots of fun because they were all so much happier. The children were working hard because they enjoyed their lessons and were doing really well at school. What a great place to be and even better was the fact that the children had done this all by themselves using their own magic. How clever was that!

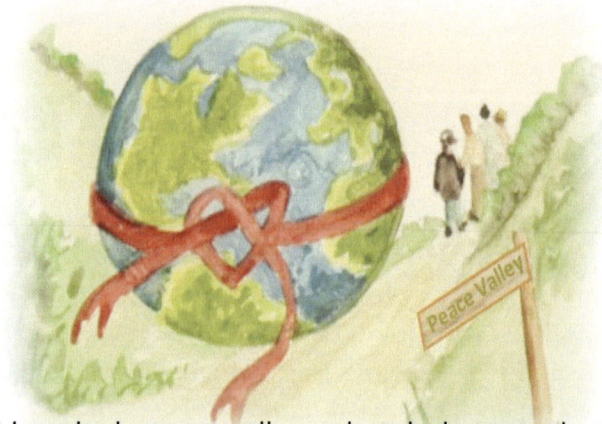

Now these children had some really cool and clever tools to use tapping and breathing. Knowing how to breathe properly and doing the Dragons Breath was brilliant. It made them laugh! And then there was their magic! All they had to do was tap into their magic on the special points and let go of any bad feelings. How clever were all these children.

When they were older and started to leave the village to have their own lives, they knew they could pass on the Dragons Breath and the Magic of Tapping to all the other people they met. They knew how this would help everyone. If everyone did Dragons Breath and tapped into their magic what a great world they would live in!

Magic of Tapping

Note to teachers, parents and carers

This story is based on a technique known as Emotional Freedom Technique (EFT) created by Gary Craig. It is known as a meridian based energy therapy. The technique works with acupuncture points and can provide rapid relief from physical pain and emotional issues such as fear, anger, sadness etc. It can also clear negative thoughts that block our potential thereby enabling us to achieve more in any area of life.

While EFT has produced some great results in clinical trials it is not intended to replace any medical treatment by a qualified medical practitioner or mental health professional. The tapping procedure described below can be helpful for your student or child. However if you have any concerns please consult a medical practitioner before using this technique.

Penny Rush is an Advanced EFT Practitioner and is registered with the Association for the Advancement of Meridian Energy Technique. For more information regarding EFT workshops please visit www.happyandhealthyminds.com.

How to tap into your magic:

Decide what the bad feeling is that you want to tap away and name the feeling.

Then gently tap on the side of your hand with two fingers and repeat this statement three times:

"Even though I have this .... (sadness, anger, pain etc) I'm really ok." Then tap on each of the following acupuncture points while talking about the bad feeling:

1. Top of the head
2. Beginning of the eyebrow
3. Side of the eye
4. Under the eye
5. Under the nose
6. Middle of the chin
7. Next to collarbone
8. Under the armpit
Then take a deep breath

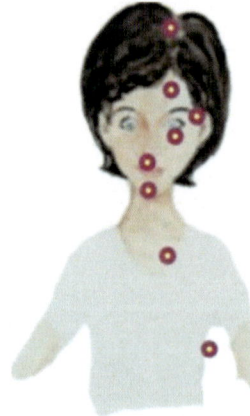

You can tap with either hand or either side of the face it doesn't matter which, the magic still works. You can tap several rounds to help you feel better. Just remember to tap into the magic every time you feel sad, bad, miserable, cross or angry with someone; it will help you to feel better!

Dragons Breath

Note to teachers, parents and carers

This story is based on a technique known as 7th Level Breathing created by Linda Graham which she has been teaching for over fifteen years. This breathing technique helps you to find instant stress relief and to conquer fear. It is a very helpful tool to clear blocks in your emotional field. Breathing is something that generally goes on in the background of our lives and yet we pay little attention to it.

7th Level Breathing helps with: Stress, Anxiety, Depression, Insomnia, Fear, Patience, Confidence, Creativity, Relationships, Change, Spiritual Journeys, Meditation, IBS, Tension, Relaxation, Life and so much more.

We all experience stressful moments in our lives and learning techniques to manage stress is beneficial. During her 7th Level Breathing workshop, Linda teaches how we can have an understanding of our breath patterns and how our thoughts have a direct link with our breathing. In this workshop you can learn how you can use your breathing to change how to react to everything. 7th Level Breathing helps you to be more conscious about your breathing and even just one conscious breath a day will change your life.

While Dragons Breath is very beneficial it is not intended to replace any medical treatment by a qualified medical practitioner or mental health professional. The Dragons Breath approach described in the story can be helpful for your student or child. However if you have any concerns please consult a medical practitioner before using this technique.

Linda Graham Atma IHM is a mother of four sons and has twelve grandchildren. Linda is a practising Reiki Master, International Spiritual Teacher, Indian Head Massage Tutor, Astrologer and Spiritual Artist. For more information please visit www.lindagraham.eu

Dragons Breath and The Magic of Tapping evolved when the authors Linda and Penny met whilst working at a Primary Head Teachers Conference. They started talking about therapies and how they could best help children. The idea developed into workshops and this book aimed at Primary School aged children.